ROOTED IN CHRIST

A 30-Day Devotional on Your True Identity

ROOTED IN CHRIST

— A 30-Day Devotional on Your True Identity —

Erick Hurt

**GOSPEL
SUPPORT**
PUBLISHING

Why One Devotional a Day?

This devotional was intentionally designed to be read one lesson per day. Not because the content is long, but because the goal is depth. True spiritual transformation doesn't come through quickly consuming truths but through slowing down and allowing the Holy Spirit to do His work in the heart.

Each day's reading is meant to be meditated on, prayed through, and lived out. Reflection questions are included not to fill time, but to create space for meditation, clarity, and response. When we rush past truth, we often miss its transforming power. When we slow down, the Lord has room to reveal, renew, and refine.

This pace also gives opportunity to grow in self-control, one of the beautiful fruits of the Spirit (Galatians 5:22–23). Holding back the urge to move ahead—even when it's "just one more"—shows the maturity and growth needed to lead others in Christ. So resist the urge to hurry. Take your time. And let each day's lesson linger.

Using This Devotional in a Group Setting

This 30-day devotional was designed not only for personal growth, but also to support group study and discussion. If you're going through this with a small group, Bible study, or church class, you'll find a simple **Leader's Guide** at the back of this book.

The Leader's Guide includes:

- A suggested weekly group format

- Discussion prompts for each devotional

- Application questions to help your group reflect and respond

- Space for additional notes and insights

Whether you're leading two people or twenty, this guide will help you keep the focus on Christ and make space for real connection and transformation.

Table of Contents

Day 1 – Psalm 1:5-6
Sinner or Saint? 1

Day 2 – Romans 6:6-7
Dead to Sin, Alive in Christ..............................5

Day 3 – 1 Corinthians 15:3-4
Redefined by the Gospel...................................9

Day 4 – John 10:27-30
Safe and Secure..13

Day 5 – Ephesians 1:13-14
Sealed and Guaranteed....................................17

Day 6 – Ezekiel 36:26
Do I Have a New or Wicked Heart?...................21

Day 7 – Romans 3:23-24
All Have Sinned and Fall Short, Right?...............25

Day 8 – Hebrews 10:14
Confessing To Every Sin Every Time?................29

Day 9 – 2 Corinthians 3:3
Tablets of Stone and The Law of Liberty..............33

Day 10 – Colossians 2:13-14
I Don't Feel Forgiven.......................................37

Day 11 – Matthew 11:28-30
    Trying Harder vs. Resting in Christ.........................41

Day 12 – Galatians 5:17
    It Feels Like I Still Want to Sin.............................45

Day 13 – Romans 13:10
    The Moral Law vs. The Law of Love.....................49

Day 14 – 2 Corinthians 5:21
    Righteousness or Worthlessness?...........................53

Day 15 – John 6:37
    Will I Be Cast Out of God's Presence?...................57

Day 16 – Romans 8:1
    Will Believers Be Judged and Condemned?.............61

Day 17 – Isaiah 53:5
    Forensic Files and the Wounds of Christ.................65

Day 18 – Ephesians 5:27
    Am I the Ugliest Bride?..69

Day 19 – 1 Thessalonians 5:9
    Is God Mad at Me Every Time I Sin?.....................73

Day 20 – Matthew 7:23
    Will God Tell Me, 'Depart from Me?'.....................77

Day 21 – Psalm 103:12
    My Sins Run Too Deep and Wide...........................81

Day 22 – Hebrews 12:4

    Am I a Hypocrite?.......................................85

Day 23 – Luke 18:1

    But I'm Not a "Prayer Warrior"..................89

Day 24 – Psalm 61:3

    Do I Spend Enough Time with God?...........93

Day 25 – Romans 6:23

    The Wages of Sin vs. The Gift of God...................97

Day 26 – Romans 15:7

    I Feel Unaccepted in God's Sight........................101

Day 27 – John 5:24

    Should I Be Afraid of Hell?........................105

Day 28 – Ephesians 1:4

    Holy and Blameless..109

Day 29 – Ephesians 1:5

    Adopted and Loved..113

Day 30 – Romans 8:38-39

    Nothing Can Separate Us................................117

Introduction

Rooted in Christ: A 30-Day Devotional on Your True Identity

Who are you, really?

That question may seem simple, but for many believers, the answer is clouded by past mistakes, current struggles, or future fears. Too often, we define ourselves by what we've done, what others have said, or how we feel in the moment. But none of these things can tell us the truth about who we are in Christ.

This devotional is written to help you plant your feet firmly in what God says about you. If you have placed your faith in Jesus, your old identity is gone—and your new identity is secure, unshakable, and rooted in Christ.

But being "in Christ" isn't just a spiritual label. It's a daily reality meant to reshape how you think, feel, and live. When you know who you are, you'll finally understand how to walk in the freedom and purpose God designed for you.

Each of the next 30 days focuses on a key gospel truth about your identity—truths drawn straight from the Bible. You'll find:

- A title to anchor the theme

- A Bible verse or passage to meditate on

- A short devotional to guide your thinking

- Reflection questions to apply what you've read

- A prayer to express your heart to God

This journey is not about trying harder. It's about believing and resting in who you are. Transformation flows from the inside out—when the gospel takes root in your heart, it produces fruit in your life.

Take it one day at a time. Ask the Holy Spirit to help you receive, rest in, and rejoice in the truth. You don't need to become someone new. You already are.

Day 1 – Sinner or Saint?

Truth for Today: Psalm 1:5–6

"Therefore the wicked will not stand in the judgment, nor sinners in the assembly of the righteous. For the Lord watches over the way of the righteous, but the way of the wicked leads to destruction."

---

*A*s a believer in Jesus Christ, how do you see yourself? Are you still a sinner—just forgiven? Or a saint who sometimes sins?

Before knowing Christ, we were dead in our sins. Sinner was not just something we did—it was who we were. But Jesus came for sinners, to save them, cleanse them, and give them a new life. The question is, should "sinner" still define us after we've been united with Christ?

Psalm 1 draws a sharp line between the wicked and the righteous. "Sinners will not stand in the judgment, nor in the assembly of the righteous." One group faces destruction; the other is watched over by the Lord. There's no mixing of categories here. There's a clear divide, sinners and saints, darkness and light, wicked and righteous.

This separation echoes throughout the New Testament. Consider 2 Corinthians 6:14: "Do not be yoked together with unbelievers. For what do righteousness and wickedness have in common? Or what fellowship can light have with darkness?"

These verses show the spiritual reality of two opposing identities. Righteousness and wickedness have nothing in common. The gospel didn't just provide forgiveness; it transferred us from one realm to another. You were once in darkness—now you are light in the Lord (Ephesians 5:8).

This is why "sinner" no longer fits with who you are in Christ. Jesus, the perfect sacrifice, became sin for you—so that you might become the righteousness of God in Him (2 Corinthians 5:21). He bore your judgment. He died your death. And He raised you up as He was raised from the grave to give you His life.

Now, you are a new creation (2 Corinthians 5:17). You are not a sinner struggling to become holy. You are holy, learning to live as one who is already set apart. Yes, you still stumble. But your identity isn't defined by your failure—it's defined by your union with Christ.

The gospel doesn't just cleanse your record—it changes your nature.

So today, embrace who you are in Christ. Stop calling yourself what Jesus died for, and put to death. You are not "just a sinner." You are a saint—redeemed, righteous, and deeply loved.

Prayer

Father, thank You that in Christ I am no longer a sinner, but a saint. Help me to live from my new identity—not out of guilt, but through Your grace provided to me. Let the truth of who I am in Jesus shape everything I think, say, and do.

Reflection Questions

1. In your heart and your language, do you still identify more with who you were—or with who you now are in Christ?

2. How does seeing yourself as a saint who sometimes sins (instead of a sinner who sometimes does good) change the way you approach God?

3. What area of your life would look different if you fully believed your identity as "the righteousness of God in Christ?"

_____

_____

_____

_____

_____

_____

_____

_____

_____

_____

_____

_____

_____

Day 2 – Dead to Sin, Alive in Christ

Truth for Today: Romans 6:5–7

"For if we have been united with him in a death like his, we will certainly also be united with him in a resurrection like his. For we know that our old self was crucified with him so that the body ruled by sin might be done away with, that we should no longer be slaves to sin—because anyone who has died has been set free from sin."

---

*M*any believers struggle with the thought of the old and new self. Some may say that I still need to "die to self" and "crucify" the old man. But Romans 6 clearly says that our "old self" that was "ruled by sin" was "done away with"—(past tense) "crucified." And the results were as clear as day—you were "set free" from your slavery to sin. Now that is some good news!

Jesus came to set captives free—not just to forgive your past, but to break the power of sin in your present.

Before knowing Christ, you weren't someone who sometimes sinned—you were a slave to sin. No matter how hard you tried, you couldn't escape the "rule of sin" over your life. But Romans 6 declares something amazing—some truly good news: your old self—the sinful, enslaved version of you—was crucified with Christ. You are not just improved; you are not just forgiven and sent back to try harder—but you have been crucified with Christ!

And if your old self died with Jesus then you've also been raised with Him. Resurrection isn't just a future hope. It's your current spiritual reality. You have a new life because you've been made new from the inside out.

Other messages will tell you to work harder to please God. Try harder. Do better. Keep the rules. But all that striving is just behavior management, or modification, not real transformation. It's focused on the outside. The gospel is greater! The gospel says: You died. You were buried. You were raised to life.

You don't obey in order to be free, you obey because you *are* free.

This is why the Christian life is not about trying to become something. It's about believing who you already are in Christ. That truth inspires real transformation—because it doesn't come from self-effort, but from your union with Jesus.

So when temptation calls, or sin whispers that you're still trapped, or you think it's the "old self" calling from the grave, you can say with full confidence: "My old self died…anyone who has died has been set free from sin."

Prayer

Father, thank You that my old self was crucified and raised with Christ, and therefore no longer a slave to sin. Help me believe this truth and walk in the freedom Jesus already purchased for me.

Reflection Questions

1. Are you living like your old self is still alive—or are you believing that Christ has already set you free?

_____

_____

_____

_____

2. How does knowing your old self was crucified with Christ change the way you face temptation today?

_____

_____

_____

_____

3. In what areas of your life do you still live as if sin has power over you–and how can you start walking in the freedom Jesus already secured?

_____

_____

_____

_____

_____

_____

_____

_____

_____

_____

_____

_____

Day 3 – Redefined by the Gospel

Truth for Today: 1 Corinthians 15:3–4

"For what I received I passed on to you as of first importance: that Christ died for our sins according to the Scriptures, that he was buried, that he was raised on the third day according to the Scriptures."

---

*P*aul opens his message to the Corinthians with what he calls the matter of first importance, the gospel.

This wasn't just a theological statement—it was a deep truth that became very personal. Paul had once been Saul, a religious zealot who persecuted Christians. But when he believed the gospel, everything changed—his identity, purpose, and future. The murderer became a missionary. The slanderer of Christ became a servant of Christ.

This same gospel is what redefines us today.

We are not defined by our past, our failures, or even our efforts to do better. We are defined by what Jesus did for us—His death, burial, and resurrection. As Paul says, Christ died for our sins; He was buried, and He was raised on the third day. This is the good news that changes everything—not just where we go when we die, but who we are while we live.

Romans 5:19 explains it clearly:

> *"For just as through the disobedience of the one man the many were made sinners, so also through the obedience of the one man the many will be made righteous."*

Adam's disobedience made us sinners. We inherited that nature, and with it, the penalty of death. But Jesus' obedience—even unto death on a cross—made us righteous. Not because of our effort. Not because we cleaned ourselves up. But because of His perfect obedience on our behalf.

This is your new identity: righteous in Christ. Forgiven and loved by God. Set free from sin. Not because you earned or deserved it, but because Jesus finished it. It's no wonder the gospel is called "good news!"

You've been transferred from death to life, from guilt to grace, and from sinner to saint. Yes—you! Not merely someday in heaven, but right now, in Christ.

Look how Paul addresses the early believers:

- *"To all those in Rome who are loved by God and called to be saints..."* (Romans 1:7)

- *"To those sanctified in Christ Jesus, called to be saints..."* (1 Corinthians 1:2)

- *"With all the saints..."* (2 Corinthians 1:1)

- *"To the saints who are in Ephesus..."* (Ephesians 1:1)

If you belong to Jesus, this includes you! You are a saint—set apart, sanctified, and in right standing with God because of Jesus.

Prayer

Jesus, thank You for Your obedience that made me righteous. I praise You that I am no longer a sinner in Your eyes, but a saint who has been set apart by Your grace. Help me live in that truth today.

Reflection Questions

1. Do you believe God calls you a saint? Why is it hard to believe that sometimes?

_____

_____

_____

2. How would your daily life look different if you truly saw yourself as righteous and set apart in Christ?

_____

_____

_____

_____

_____

3. What past labels or failures still try to define you—and how does the truth of the gospel redefine them?

_____

_____

_____

_____

_____

Day 4 – Safe and Secure?

Truth for Today: John 10:27–30

"My sheep listen to my voice; I know them, and they follow me. I give them eternal life, and they shall never perish; no one will snatch them out of my hand. My Father, who has given them to me, is greater than all; no one can snatch them out of my Father's hand. I and the Father are one."

Numerous Christians wrestle with fear: "Am I really safe in Christ? Or am I only secure as long as I perform well?" Proverbs reminds us that the fear of the Lord adds length to life (Proverbs 10:27), and there is a right kind of reverence we're meant to walk in. But fear is never meant to be a source of insecurity about our salvation.

Some live as though their safety in Christ is temporary—strong when they're doing well, fragile when they fall short. But the Bible is clear: we are not secure because of how well we perform; we are secure because of what Christ has already accomplished. The blood of Jesus didn't purchase conditional safety. It purchased and secured eternal life.

In John 10, Jesus says plainly: *"I give them eternal life, and they shall never perish."*

Think about it! They shall *never* perish! Jesus isn't describing temporary life. It's not a trial period. It's eternal life!

His life—and it can never be lost. Romans 6:9 reminds us that Christ, being raised from the dead, "can never die again." And because we now share in His life, we will never perish.

What does Jesus give to His sheep that will never perish? Eternal life, which isn't your life made longer? Wait what? Yes, that's right, it's not your life made longer, Jesus is life and the One who is eternal. You have His life living in you and because He lives you will live also.

This is the way to embrace what eternal life really means. So now think of how secure your identity really is! It's built on the solid Rock where we stand—rooted in Jesus' finished work.

Look at the two hands holding you, shielding you, loving you and embracing you. You are in the most secure place in the entire universe, protected by hands from which you can never be snatched! Jesus' nail-scarred hand, and the Father's hand.

Can anything be more secure than that? The Son holds us. The Father holds us. And no one—not sin, not Satan, not even our failures—can snatch us from their grip. Our security doesn't rest in our grip on God, but in His grip on us.

That's why the fear of the Lord isn't about terror or insecurity. It's about reverence for the One who gave everything to secure us forever. We don't live afraid of being cast out—we live in awe of the grace that brought us near.

Prayer

Father, thank You that my life is hidden in Christ and held in Your hand. I rest today in the promise that no one can snatch me from You and Your Son who hold me. Help me walk in that confidence today, rather than in fear of judgment.

Reflection Questions

1. Are you living with peace in your security in Christ—or with fear that you could lose it?

_____

_____

_____

_____

2. How does knowing that your life is held in both the Father's and the Son's hands change the way you face trials or failures?

_____

_____

_____

3. What would it look like for you to live each day
   from a place of confidence instead of fear—fully
   trusting that Jesus will never let you go?

Day 5 – Sealed and Guaranteed

Truth for Today: Ephesians 1:13–14

"And you also were included in Christ when you heard the message of truth, the gospel of your salvation. When you believed, you were marked in him with a seal, the promised Holy Spirit, who is a deposit guaranteeing our inheritance..."

---

*I*f God says you're sealed, who could possibly break that seal?

When you believed the gospel, something miraculous happened. Not only were you forgiven and made righteous–you were also marked, sealed, and guaranteed by the Holy Spirit. Ephesians 1 says when you heard the message of truth and believed it, you were included in Christ and sealed by the Holy Spirit.

The word "seal" in the ancient world signified ownership, authenticity, and security. Kings would seal documents with a signet ring—stamping their authority and guaranteeing the contents. If anyone tampered with the seal, they were defying the king himself.

So what does it mean that you've been sealed by God with the Holy Spirit? It means no one can tamper with God's seal on you. It is the most costly seal ever–one that cost Jesus His life. And after He rose from the grave, He promised to send the Holy Spirit "to be with you forever" (John 14:16). Your identity, inheritance, and eternal destiny have been secured by His divine authority. You belong to God now—He has stamped His name on your life.

Even more, the Bible says the Holy Spirit is a deposit guaranteeing your inheritance. God didn't just promise you eternal life–He gave you the first taste of it now. The Spirit in you is heaven's down payment, and God never makes payments He plans to cancel.

Some fear that they might lose the Spirit if they sin or fall short. But think about it: if the Spirit is part of the free gift of salvation, and that gift is what guarantees your future with God–how could He be taken away?

The Spirit isn't a temporary companion or a silent partner. He is your guarantee, your seal, your eternal Comforter, Counselor, Helper, and the One who guides you into all truth (John 16:13). Jesus said the Holy Spirit would be with us forever–not until we sin, not until we struggle, but forever!

This is why the gospel brings rest. You don't have to hold it all together. You are held by the Spirit. You are safe, marked, known, and secure–not because of how tightly you cling to God, but because of the unbreakable seal of the Holy Spirit.

Prayer

Father, thank You for sealing me with the Holy Spirit when I believed. Thank You that I am Yours forever. Help me rest in the truth that my salvation is guaranteed—not by my grip on You, but by Your Spirit in me.

Reflection Questions

1. Do you live like someone who is sealed by God and guaranteed eternal life?

_____

_____

_____

_____

2. How does knowing the Holy Spirit is God's seal of ownership on your life affect the way you see yourself each day?

_____

_____

_____

_____

3. When doubts or fears about your salvation arise, how can remembering the Spirit's unbreakable seal bring you back to peace and assurance?

_____

_____

_____

_____

_____

_____

_____

_____

_____

_____

_____

_____

_____

Day 6 – Do I Have a New or Wicked Heart?

Truth for Today: Ezekiel 36:26

"I will give you a new heart and put a new spirit in you; I will remove from you your heart of stone and give you a heart of flesh."

$\mathcal{R}$emember the Bible verse, "The heart is deceitful above all things" (Jeremiah 17:9)? It's often quoted by pastors or leaders to remind us of how sinful we are—an attempt to motivate believers. But what if you've been made new and given a new heart? Does that description still apply to a believer in Christ?

According to the Bible, no.

Before Christ, yes—our hearts were hardened, rebellious, and wicked. We were dead in our sins, unable to please God, and deceived by our desires. But God made a promise through the prophet Ezekiel that He would do something so powerful for His people:

"I will give you a new heart... I will remove your heart of stone and give you a heart of flesh."

That's not wishful thinking, but a spiritual reality for every believer. When you trusted in Jesus, you didn't just get a fresh start—you got a new heart. On the cross He breathed out His last breath so you could take your first breath as a new creation. On the cross His heart was pierced but you received a new one—becoming a new creation.

You're not living with a divided, deceitful heart that secretly wants to run from God. You're living with a new heart that loves God, one that is responsive to Him and desires what He desires. That's what it means to be "born again." The old is gone, the new has come (2 Corinthians 5:17).

Let me be clear, you still have those old patterns of thinking running through your mind. But your heart of stone was removed and God gave you a new heart of flesh. Your former heart was hard like stone. It was cold, hard, and callous. But with your new heart of flesh, you can love, care for, and forgive others. Not perfectly, but as you learn, grow, and practice.

To say your heart is wicked after salvation is to deny the miracle God performed in you. The transformation is real—even if you're still learning to live from it. And besides, God does not give evil gifts or wicked hearts to His children.

You may still sin, but your new heart is not at home with sin. You grieve over it, you change your mind regarding it, and you return to your senses so you can escape from it. That's not the sign of a wicked heart—it's the sign of a heart made alive by the Spirit of God.

This truth changes everything. You don't need to beg God to give you a clean heart—He already has. You don't need to live in suspicion of your motives—you can walk in confidence that your heart now beats in a spiritual rhythm with His.

Prayer

Father, thank You for taking out my heart of stone and giving me a heart of flesh. Thank You for making me new. Help me live from my new heart, trusting that I now desire what You desire.

Reflection Questions

1. Do you see yourself as someone with a new heart that loves God and others?

_____

_____

_____

_____

2. When you struggle with sin or failure, do you respond as someone with a wicked heart trying to earn God's love, or as someone with a new heart learning to live in His grace?

_____

_____

_____

3. How can trusting that God has already given you a new heart change the way you respond, think, and relate to others this week?

Day 7 – All Have Sinned and Fall Short, Right?

Truth for Today: Romans 3:23–24

"For all have sinned and fall short of the glory of God, and all are justified freely by his grace through the redemption that came by Christ Jesus."

---

*Y*ou've probably heard it a thousand times: "We all fall short." It's usually said with a shrug—an attempt to explain ongoing sin or failure. And yes, Romans 3:23 does say that "all have sinned and fall short of the glory of God."

But don't stop reading there.

Verse 24 continues: "and ALL are justified freely by his grace through the redemption that came by Christ Jesus." Even the word 'redemption' reminds us of the power of His blood— RED-EMPTI-ON.

Romans 3:23 is not describing the identity of a believer; it's describing the condition of all humanity apart from Christ. That was us before salvation—guilty, falling short, and without hope. But once we put our faith in Jesus, everything changed.

We are no longer defined by verse 23. We are now defined by verse 24.

You have been justified—declared righteous by God. You have been redeemed—bought back by the blood of Jesus. You have freely received God's grace—given a new standing, a new heart, and a new identity. Yes, all have sinned—past tense, "have" sinned. But that's not who you are anymore.

We should never use Romans 3:23 to describe a believer's ongoing identity. In fact, chapter after chapter, Romans calls believers "saints," "righteous," "alive in Christ," "slaves to righteousness," and "new creations." You are not someone who is still falling short—you are someone who has been lifted up by the grace of God.

So what happens when you stumble? Does that mean you've fallen short again and need to get re-justified? Not at all. The gospel doesn't fluctuate with your performance. When Jesus redeemed you, He did it fully and forever. You're not on probation with God.

Yes, you may fall into sin, but you no longer live in sin. You no longer identify as a sinner falling short—you are a redeemed child of God walking in grace. And when you fall, His grace picks you back up.

Let's stop using Romans 3:23 as a way to excuse failure or deny the power of the new life we've been given. Instead, let's rejoice and remember Romans 3:24—the unshakable truth that we've been justified freely by His grace, and that His RED-EMPTI-ON has made us white as snow (Isaiah 1:18).

Prayer

Father, thank You that I am no longer defined by my past or by falling short. I am justified, redeemed, and made new in Christ. Help me live from that truth today and not from old patterns or old labels.

Reflection Questions

1. Have you been using Romans 3:23 to describe yourself—even though you've been justified by grace?

_____

_____

_____

_____

2. How does knowing you are fully justified and redeemed change how you see your daily struggles?

_____

_____

_____

_____

3. What would it look like to live from verse 24 instead of verse 23 today?

_____

_____

_____

_____

_____

_____

_____

_____

_____

_____

_____

_____

_____

Day 8 – Confessing Every Sin Every Time?

Truth for Today: Hebrews 10:14

"For by one sacrifice he has made perfect forever those who are being made holy."

$\mathcal{M}$any believers live with a low-grade anxiety that if they forget to confess a sin, they'll somehow fall out of favor with God—or worse, be in danger of judgment. But that's not what the gospel teaches—it's much better.

Do you need to confess every single sin, every single time, in order to remain forgiven and right with God? The truth is, you were not forgiven because you remembered every sin. You were forgiven because Jesus died for sin once and for all—past, present, and future.

Hebrews 10:14 says:

"For by one sacrifice he has made perfect forever those who are being made holy."

Let that sink in. One sacrifice. Made perfect. Forever. That means your standing with God isn't dependent on your ability to keep perfect records—it's based on Jesus' finished work. At the cross, Jesus didn't just offer partial cleansing or conditional forgiveness. He offered a once-for-all sacrifice that completely dealt with sin.

Confession for the believer is no longer a means of getting clean—it's a way of walking with God with thanksgiving. It's relational, not transactional. You're not confessing in hopes that God will forgive you—you're confessing because you know He already has.

1 John 1:9 says, "If we confess our sins, He is faithful and just to forgive us our sins and cleanse us from all unrighteousness." This verse is about receiving salvation and it comes with the cleansing of all unrighteousness. You're not confessing every sin to be more forgiven; we've already received total forgiveness (Hebrews 10:14).

When we confess, we're not asking God to do something—He already has. We're simply agreeing with Him about what's true. Did you hear that? We're walking in the light, receiving fresh grace, and delighting our hearts with the truth of the gospel.

Think about this: Do you really believe you could remember and confess every single sin you commit—every wrong thought, every bad attitude, every selfish motive? Of course not. But thankfully, your forgiveness isn't based on your memory or your confessions—it's based on Christ's blood and righteousness.

So live free, agree freely, and rejoice that all of your sin has been dealt with, past, present, and future. Therefore, let us agree with God that Jesus' blood is more powerful than the sin He came to die for.

Prayer

Father, thank You that my forgiveness is not based on my performance or my memory, but on Jesus' once-for-all sacrifice. Help me walk in the light, quick to confess (agree with You)—not to be forgiven, but because I already am.

Reflection

1. Have you been confessing your sins out of fear or out of freedom?

_____

_____

_____

_____

2. How are you resting in the once-for-all sacrifice of Jesus?

_____

_____

_____

_____

_____

3. What would it look like to fully embrace that all of your sin has been completely paid for, past, present and future?

_____

_____

_____

_____

_____

_____

_____

_____

_____

_____

_____

_____

_____

Day 9 – Tablets of Stone and the Law of Liberty

Truth for Today: 2 Corinthians 3:3

"You show that you are a letter from Christ… not written with ink but with the Spirit of the living God, not on tablets of stone but on tablets of human hearts."

That was the limitation of the Old Covenant.. Rules can shape behavior—but they can't change hearts. God gave His people the law, written on tablets of stone. These commandments were holy, just, and good—but they couldn't make people holy, just, or good. They exposed sin but offered no power to overcome it. They demanded obedience but gave no help to obey. The law was perfect—but we were not.

But then something incredible happened. In Christ, a new covenant began—sealed in His blood, and written not on stone, but on the tablets of human hearts. 2 Corinthians 3 says, "You are a letter from Christ… written by the Spirit of the living God." You are no longer defined by what the law points out. You are defined by what the Spirit has written within.

This is not self-improvement. It's a miracle of transformation. The law carved in stone said, "You must become righteous." But the Spirit in your heart says, "You've been made righteous—now walk in it."

You no longer live under a system that brings condemnation and death (2 Corinthians 3:6–9). You live under the law of liberty—a law that gives life and freedom. As James 1:25 says, this law is perfect because it flows from a perfect Savior who fulfilled every demand in your place.

Jesus obeyed the law fully—and bore its curse completely—so you wouldn't have to live under fear or failure. The pressure to perform is gone. The weight of guilt is lifted. In its place is the empowering presence of the Spirit, writing truth on your heart and leading you into a life filled with love and joy.

The old law says, "Do this or die."

The gospel says, "Jesus died for you. It is finished—now live."

You're not just forgiven—you're free. You're not trying to earn God's approval—you already have it. And now, the same Spirit who engraved grace on your heart empowers you to live it out.

Prayer

Father, thank You for taking away the weight of the law and writing Your truth on my heart. Thank You for giving me the Spirit of life and liberty. Help me walk in freedom—not out of obligation, but as a response to Your grace and love.

Reflection Questions

1. Are you living under the pressure of external performance—or the freedom of Spirit-empowered transformation?

_____

_____

_____

_____

_____

2. Do you view God's commands as burdens to bear—or as invitations to walk in your new identity?

_____

_____

_____

_____

_____

3. How does it make you feel that you are not under the law written on tablets of stone, but under God's grace by the Spirit who wrote His law of liberty on your heart?

_____

_____

_____

_____

_____

_____

_____

_____

_____

_____

_____

_____

_____

Day 10 – I Don't Feel Forgiven

Truth for Today: Colossians 2:13–14

"When you were dead in your sins and in the uncircumcision of your flesh, God made you alive with Christ. He forgave us all our sins, having canceled the charge of our legal indebtedness... he has taken it away, nailing it to the cross."

---

*I*t's one thing to believe that God forgives sins. It's another thing to feel forgiven. Some days guilt still lingers. Regret can resurface like an old wound. And when that happens, it's easy to wonder, Did God really forgive me? or Why don't I feel clean?

But forgiveness isn't a feeling. It's a fact grounded in the finished work of Christ.

Colossians 2 says that when you were dead in sin, God made you alive with Christ. Not only that—He forgave all your sins. Not just the ones you confessed. Not just the ones you regret the most. But all of them.

And how did He do it?

By taking the full list of your sins—your "legal indebtedness"—and nailing it to the cross. That means the record of wrongs that stood against you was publicly and permanently displayed in Christ and removed from you. Your sins weren't swept under the rug. They were nailed to a Roman cross and buried in a tomb that Jesus left empty.

So why don't we always feel forgiven?

Often, it's because we're still looking inward—evaluating our feelings, our behavior, or our performance instead of trusting the gospel that saved us. But our forgiveness is not based on our performance or our feelings. It's based on God's promise and Christ's blood.

When Jesus cried out, "It is finished," He meant it. He didn't say, "It's almost finished, but you need to feel bad long enough to seal the deal." He didn't say, "You're forgiven as long as you keep proving yourself." No—He finished the work once for all.

The enemy loves to stir doubt by pointing you back to your sins. But the Holy Spirit always points you back to the cross. When you don't feel forgiven, it's not time to wallow in shame. It's time to remember what God did for you and in you.

When you were dead, God made you alive, He forgave all of your sins, and canceled the charge of your legal indebtedness! By nailing it all to the cross in Jesus' flesh. It truly is finished! Now it's time to live free and fully forgiven!

Prayer

Father, thank You that my forgiveness is complete—not because of how I feel, but because of what Jesus has done. When guilt creeps in, remind me of the cross and resurrection. Help me walk in the freedom You already secured for me.

Reflection Questions

1. Have you been trusting your feelings more than God's Word when it comes to forgiveness? Why or why not?

_____

_____

_____

_____

_____

2. What helps you remember the finished work of Christ and stay rooted and grounded in it?

_____

_____

_____

_____

3. How did Colossians 2 speak to your heart today? What will change as a result of today's devotional?

_____

_____

_____

_____

_____

_____

_____

_____

_____

_____

_____

Day 11 – Trying Harder vs. Resting in Christ

Truth for Today: Matthew 11:28–30

"Come to me, all you who are weary and burdened, and I will give you rest. Take my yoke upon you and learn from me, for I am gentle and humble in heart, and you will find rest for your souls. For my yoke is easy and my burden is light."

---

*H*ave you ever felt like being a "good Christian" is exhausting? Like you're constantly striving to do more, sin less, pray longer, serve harder—yet still feel like you're falling short?

If so, you're not alone. Jesus never called us to live the Christian life in our own strength. He invites us into rest—not in passivity, but in dependence. His rest isn't inactivity; it's trust.

In Matthew 11, Jesus offers rest to the weary. He's not speaking to the rebellious or indifferent, but to those who are trying hard—religiously, morally, spiritually—but finding no rest, and no peace. They're carrying burdens they were never meant to bear.

Jesus says, "Come to me… and I will give you rest."

Too many Christians live as if the weight of the Christian life is on their shoulders. They try harder, promise to do more, rededicate again and again, and end up burned out. But the gospel is not about trying harder, promising more, or rededicating over and over—it's about trusting the One who can give you the rest and peace you're looking for.

Resting in Christ means believing that He really is enough—that His life in you is your source of strength, joy, and peace. It's not about how committed you are to Him, but how He has completely committed Himself to you.

This doesn't mean we stop learning and growing. But it does mean we stop striving in our own effort to become what only Christ has and can make us. It means we no longer live for God as if He's distant—we live from God, who lives within.

Galatians puts it this way;

> *"I have been crucified with Christ and I no longer live, but Christ lives in me..." (Galatians 2:20)*

Trying harder says, "I need to do this on my own." Resting in Christ says, "I can do all things through Him who strengthens me." One leads to exhaustion, pride, or despair. The other leads to peace, dependence, and real fruitfulness.

When we rest in Christ, we're not giving up—we're giving in. Giving in to the truth that we are already accepted, forgiven, and empowered by His Spirit. Are you weary and burdened? Come to Jesus, who said "I will give you rest."

Prayer

Jesus, thank You that Your yoke is easy and Your burden is light. Help me to rest in Your perfect offering and finished work. I don't want to live by my own strength but through Your life in me. Help me walk in faith, be at peace, and find my total rest in You.

Reflection Questions

1. Are you trying harder to live for God—or resting in the truth that Christ lives in you?

_____

_____

_____

_____

2. Where in your life are you striving instead of resting?

_____

_____

_____

_____

3. What would it look like to fully rest in Jesus' finished work?

_____

_____

_____

_____

_____

_____

_____

_____

_____

_____

_____

_____

_____

_____

Day 12 – It Feels Like I Still Want to Sin

Truth for Today: Galatians 5:17

"For the desires of the flesh are against the Spirit, and the desires of the Spirit are against the flesh, for these are opposed to each other, to keep you from doing the things you want to do."

---

*H*ave you ever thought, If I'm a new creation, why do I still feel pulled toward sin? If you've asked that question, you're not alone. It can be confusing: you've been given a new heart, set free from sin, and filled with the Spirit—so why do you still feel the tension?

The Bible gives us the answer in Galatians 5:17. There's a conflict going on—not between two equal parts of who you are, but between the true you in Christ, and those lingering influencers with their patterns and practices, or you might call them "old habits."

Let's make something clear: your heart is new. Your spirit is new. And God lives in you. God did not leave you with a deceitful heart (Jeremiah 17:9 describes your heart before Christ). Ezekiel 36:26 says He removed your heart of stone and gave you a heart of flesh—a heart that loves Him, desires righteousness, and wants to please Him.

But you still have old thoughts, patterns, habits, and ways of coping that were trained in you before you knew Christ. All of the old you is being transformed as you learn, grow, and mature in Christ. Those old thoughts and patterns need to be denied, taken captive, and put to death (Romans 6:11). But your heart? It has already been made new.

So when you feel a pull toward sin, it's not coming from within—from your new heart—it's coming from an outside source, that *old programming*. And you are not that old person anymore. Even while struggling internally, we recognize: "That's not the real me." That's not your true self; you're the new self!

Here's the good news: you don't actually want to sin. If you're in Christ, you may feel temptation. You may stumble. But you grieve it. You hate it. That's not the desire of a wicked heart—that's the cry of a new heart that longs to walk with God in the freedom He purchased for you.

And that's exactly what the Spirit is producing in you. As you walk by the Spirit, you won't gratify the desires of the flesh (Galatians 5:16). The power of sin has been broken, and you're not obligated to obey it anymore.

You are free indeed—not from temptation, but from your slavery and bondage to sin. And every time you say no to sin, you're suppressing those old patterns, practices, and habits—and expressing your true identity with its new desires.

Prayer

Father, thank You that I have a new heart. When temptation comes, help me remember that the pull is not who I am. Teach me to walk by the Spirit and trust You moment by moment.

Reflection Questions

1. Have you confused the voice of an outside source with your true desires in Christ?

_____

_____

_____

_____

_____

2. How does knowing you have a new heart help you fight temptation differently?

_____

_____

_____

_____

3. How does knowing that you have "old" patterns, practices, and habits help with your confidence in Christ?

_____

_____

_____

_____

_____

_____

_____

_____

_____

_____

_____

_____

_____

Day 13 – The Moral Law vs. the Law of Love

Truth for Today: Romans 13:10

"Love does no harm to a neighbor. Therefore love is the fulfillment of the law."

---

 hen some believers think of the law, they immediately picture the Ten Commandments or the broader "moral law" given to Israel. These laws were holy, righteous, and good—but they were also external. They told people how to live, but they didn't give them the power to live it out.

So how are believers today supposed to relate to the moral law? Are we still under it? Are we still trying to keep it?

Romans 6:14 answers clearly;

"You are not under law but under grace." That doesn't mean lawlessness. It means you've been brought under something greater—something deeper and more powerful: the law of love.

Romans 13 says that love fulfills the law. Why? Because love leads you to do what the law always pointed to. Love doesn't steal, lie, cheat, or harm others. But love also does what the law could never do—it flows from the inside out.

Under the law, the focus was on avoiding wrong. Under love, the focus is on expressing Christ.

This doesn't mean we ignore morality. It means we no longer rely on external rules to guide our behavior—we rely on the Spirit of God and the love He poured in our hearts (Romans 5:5).

Galatians 5:22–23 tells us that the fruit of the Spirit is love, joy, peace, patience, and so on. Then Galatians says, "Against such things there is no law." Why? Because when you're walking by the Spirit and expressing His love, you're already doing what the law was pointing toward—but from a new heart, not from a list of rules carved out of stone.

Jesus summarized the entire law in two commands: Love the Lord your God with all your heart, soul, mind, and strength, and love your neighbor as yourself. (Matthew 22:37–40). He didn't lower the standard—He fulfilled it and raised it. But He also gave you a new commandment, a new heart and His Spirit so you could actually live it out.

"A new commandment I give to you, that you love one another: just as I have loved you, you also are to love one another" (John 13:34). Love is the fulfillment of the law, and Jesus' new commandment is to live as "I have loved you." Jesus loved us unto His own demise, death, and destruction. Willingly He went, like a lamb led to the slaughter.

You don't need the law written on tablets of stone. You have the commandment of love written on your new heart.

Prayer

Father, thank You for writing Your love on my heart. Help me trust the Spirit's work in me and live from love—not legalism. Let love be the fruit that fulfills my life.

Reflection Questions

1. Are you living by external rules or by the internal guidance of God's love through the Spirit?

_____

_____

_____

_____

2. How does the law of love shape your daily choices?

_____

_____

_____

_____

_____

_____

3. What are your thoughts about love being the
    fulfillment of the law?

_____

_____

_____

_____

_____

_____

_____

_____

_____

_____

_____

_____

Day 14 – Righteous or Worthless?

Truth for Today: 2 Corinthians 5:21

"God made him who had no sin to be sin for us, so that in him we might become the righteousness of God."

When you look in the mirror or review your day, do you ever feel like you fall short—like you're more worthless than worthy? It's a hard place to be, weighed down by failure, guilt, or the belief you're defined by your mistakes.

But the gospel flips this story upside down. Your worth is not based on your performance or how well you live. Instead, your worth comes from what Jesus has done for you. Jesus became sin, so you could become righteous. Jesus was pierced, so you could be whole. Jesus was judged, so you could be pardoned.

Even when you know this truth in your mind, it can be hard to believe it in your heart. You may still feel like you have to make up for the past or earn back God's approval. But the cross silences that lie. Jesus didn't just remove your sin—He replaced it with His righteousness. That means when God looks at you, He doesn't see failure or filth; He sees you through His Son's finished work. You're not halfway forgiven or mostly clean. You're completely righteous, blameless, and spotless in Christ.

2 Corinthians 5:21 tells us that God made Jesus, who was without sin, to become sin for us. Why? So that through faith in Him, we might be counted as righteous before God. This means your identity is no longer "sinner" or "worthless," but "righteous" because of Christ's perfect life and perfect offering credited to your account.

If your value depended on your own efforts, you'd always be falling short. But God's gift of righteousness is exactly that—a gift. It cannot be earned or lost by good works or failure. You are declared "not guilty" and "worthy" solely because Jesus took your place and died your death.

This truth changes everything. It means you don't have to prove your worth. You can rest in the fact that you truly are righteous by the blood of Jesus. It frees you from shame and fear, allowing you to live in confidence and gratitude.

Living from this identity means you no longer define yourself by your past mistakes or your fears about the future. Instead, you live as someone fully accepted, loved by God, and empowered by His Spirit to grow in His love.

Prayer

Father, thank You for making me righteous through Jesus' perfect sacrifice. Help me to live from this truth and not out of fear or shame. Teach me to walk confidently in the freedom You purchased for me.

Reflection Questions

1. When do you most feel worthless, and how can you remind yourself of your righteousness in Christ?

_____

_____

_____

_____

_____

2. How does knowing your righteousness is a gift change the way you approach your daily struggles?

_____

_____

_____

_____

_____

3. How does Jesus' "great exchange" on the cross (and through His resurrection) make you feel that He became sin so you could become righteous?

_____

_____

_____

_____

_____

_____

_____

_____

_____

_____

_____

_____

_____

_____

Day 15 – Will I Be Cast Out of God's Presence?

Truth for Today: John 6:37

"All that the Father gives me will come to me, and whoever comes to me I will never cast out."

One of the deepest fears many believers face is this: What if God gets tired of me? What if I mess up one too many times? Will He cast me out?

This fear often hides in the shadows of shame and failure. It whispers lies that say God is close when you're doing well, but distant—or even done with you—when you fall short.

But Jesus answers that fear with stunning clarity: "Whoever comes to me I will never cast out." Not sometimes, not unless they sin again, not as long as they prove they're serious. Just: Never!

When you came to Jesus in faith, it wasn't because you earned your place—it was because the Father drew you. And Jesus says clearly that all whom the Father gives to Him will come, and none will be rejected. Not one.

That means your security in Christ isn't based on your strength, feelings, or performance. It's based on the unbreakable promise of Jesus.

David, after his worst sin, prayed, "Do not cast me from your presence or take your Holy Spirit from me" (Psalm 51:11). But that was under the old covenant, before the cross, resurrection and the indwelling Spirit came. As a new covenant believer, you have something even greater than what David had: the abiding, indwelling presence of God Who never leaves nor forsakes you.

Jesus has promised to never leave you or forsake you. The Spirit lives in you, not as a visitor but as a permanent resident. You don't have to beg God to stay—He already promised He will.

Even when you fail, His grace remains—and when you feel far from Him, He is still near, especially to the brokenhearted. Your sin couldn't drive Him away, because He came to rescue you from your it, and the blood of Jesus that drew you near is more powerful than your sin that separated you.

Prayer

Father, thank You that in Christ I am fully accepted and forever secure. I confess my fears and doubts, and I receive the truth that You will never cast me out. Help me rest in Your promise and walk boldly in Your presence.

Reflection Questions

1. Have you ever feared that God might give up on you?

---

2. How does Jesus' promise in John 6:37 speak directly to that fear?

---

3. What would it look like to live from the confidence that you are always welcome in God's presence?

_____

_____

_____

_____

_____

_____

_____

_____

_____

_____

_____

_____

_____

Day 16 – Will Believers Be Judged and Condemned?

Truth for Today: Romans 8:1

"There is therefore now no condemnation for those who are in Christ Jesus."

$\mathcal{M}$any Christians live with a lingering fear that one day they'll stand before God and hear a verdict of condemnation. They wonder if they've done enough, changed enough, or fast enough to escape judgment.

But the gospel removes this fear completely. Romans 8:1 declaration is not vague or conditional—it's absolute:

"There is therefore now no condemnation for those who are in Christ Jesus."

Let that sink in. Not less condemnation. Not a delay of condemnation. No condemnation! None now, none later, none ever—for those who are in Christ.

Why? Because Jesus was already judged and condemned in your place. The sentence you deserved for your sin was handed down at the cross. Jesus bore it fully, satisfying justice completely, and removed every reason God could ever condemn you.

This is what the gospel means: Jesus was condemned so you could be set free. The believer will stand before God—not trembling under the threat of wrath, but clothed in the righteousness of Christ. The judgment for sin already happened at Calvary. What remains for believers is not condemnation but commendation. Not punishment, but a promise of a reward for what was done in faith.

This truth should fill your heart with confidence, not pride. It's not that you've avoided judgment because you're better than others—it's because Jesus hung in your place so you could live in the light of His finished work, fully protected and fully secure. When the enemy whispers accusations, you can point to the cross and say, "The debt has been paid." Every charge against you has been dismissed by the blood of the Lamb.

Yes, the Bible speaks of a judgment seat of Christ (2 Corinthians 5:10), but this is not a judgment for sin—it's an evaluation of how people lived on planet earth. It's a moment where our works are tested by fire, and what was done through Christ will last (1 Corinthians 3:13–15). But even in this, our foundation is secure on the Rock—Jesus Christ.

The enemy wants to keep you in fear of judgment, paralyzed by guilt and shame. But God wants you to live confidently in the truth of your salvation, justification, and sanctification. The Judge is now your Father. His Son was the suffering Savior who took your place. And the verdict is in, not guilty. Shame removed, and there is now no condemnation for those who are in Christ!

Prayer

Father, thank You that in Christ I am free from all condemnation. Help me live from that truth—not in fear, but in peace and boldness. Let my life reflect the joy of being fully accepted, completely forgiven, and always loved.

Reflection Questions

1. Have you feared future judgment or condemnation from God? Why?

_____

_____

_____

_____

2. How does Romans 8:1 change the way you view your standing before God?

_____

_____

_____

_____

_____

3. Are you living in the freedom of no
    condemnation—or still trying to earn acceptance?

_____

_____

_____

_____

_____

_____

_____

_____

_____

_____

_____

_____

_____

Day 17 – Forensic Files and the Wounds of Christ

Truth for Today: Isaiah 53:5

"But he was pierced for our transgressions, he was crushed for our iniquities; the punishment that brought us peace was on him, and by his wounds we are healed."

---

*I*f you've ever watched crime shows like Forensic Files, you know how investigators examine every detail—bloodstains, fingerprints, DNA, hair—to uncover guilt or innocence. Nothing is missed. Every speck of evidence matters.

Now imagine if all the evidence of your sin, failure, and rebellion were placed on trial. Every thought, every word, every hidden motive examined. The verdict would be clear: guilty.

But then something unexpected happens. All the evidence against you—every spiritual fiber and every human fingerprint of your guilt is gathered—then transferred to someone else, Jesus.

This is what Isaiah 53 describes. Jesus was pierced for our transgressions, He didn't have any of His own. The wounds He bore were evidence—not of His guilt, but of yours and mine.

And yet, He took them willingly, and asked Thomas to examine this evidence—His hands and His side (John 20:27).

The cross wasn't just a tragic event—it was a divine exchange. The punishment that should have landed on you fell on Him. His wounds tell a story. Every scar testifies that justice has been satisfied. Every drop of blood is proof that peace has been purchased.

If Forensic Files examined the cross, they'd find overwhelming evidence—not of your condemnation, but of your redemption. The blood that speaks a better word than guilt. It cries out, "Paid in full."

So why do we often live as if we're still under investigation? Why do we keep searching our past for more evidence of failure when Jesus already carried it all to the cross?

Your case is closed. The wounds of Christ are permanent proof of purchase. Not just that your sins were real—but that they've been fully dealt with, once and for all.

This means you don't have to live with fear, guilt, or shame. God isn't holding anything over your head. The cross was enough. The verdict is in. The evidence has been examined. The DNA didn't match; it was Jesus' blood found on the cross. You've been declared forgiven, pardoned, and healed—by the blood of His wounds.

Prayer

Jesus, thank You for taking all the evidence of my guilt and bearing it in Your body. Your wounds are proof of my purchase which gives me peace. Help me stop living under investigation and start walking in the freedom You purchased for me.

Reflection Questions

1. What "evidence" from your past are you still holding onto or afraid of?

_____

_____

_____

_____

_____

2. How do the wounds of Christ assure you that your guilt has been removed?

_____

_____

_____

_____

_____

3. What would it look like to live as someone whose case has already been closed?

_____

_____

_____

_____

_____

_____

_____

_____

_____

_____

_____

_____

_____

Day 18 – Am I the Ugliest Bride?

Truth for Today: Ephesians 5:27

"...so that He might present the church to Himself in splendor, without spot or wrinkle or any such thing, that she might be holy and without blemish."

---

*H*ave you ever looked at your life and thought, How could God possibly present or delight in me? Maybe you've imagined yourself as part of the Bride of Christ—but felt like the ugliest, most unworthy member of the wedding party.

That voice of accusation is loud, Look at your sin! Look at your weakness! Look at your mess! How could Jesus want someone like you?

But that voice isn't from God. The gospel is far better and speaks a better word.

Ephesians 5 paints a breathtaking picture of Christ's love for His Bride—the Church. He doesn't just tolerate her. He doesn't cringe when He looks at her. No, He gave Himself up for her, He cleansed her, and He is preparing her as a radiant bride to be presented to the groom.

When you look at yourself, you might still see the stains, the scars, or the things you wish you could change. But when

Jesus looks at you, He sees the beauty He created, the purity He purchased, and the love He redeemed.

You are the joy set before Him—the reason He endured the cross. The Bridegroom doesn't see a failure to fix; He sees the one He died for to make His forever.

Jesus isn't presenting you to Himself because you were already flawless. He's made you flawless by His blood through His love. He sees you not as you were in your sin, but as you are in Him—holy, without blemish, spotless in His righteousness.

You are not the bride who barely made the cut. You are the beloved, chosen, and deeply cherished bride of the Lamb who rejoices over you with singing (Zephaniah 3:17). He doesn't point out your flaws, scars, or marks—He wears them Himself as proof of purchase and love for you. He doesn't recall your sins—He cleansed you of them.

The enemy wants you to believe you're unwanted and unworthy. Jesus wants you to know you're washed, adorned, and clothed in His glory.

Yes, you still struggle. Yes, you're learning and growing. But your position is already secure. Your wedding dress isn't stained by your past—it's dazzling white because it's been washed in the blood of the Lamb.

Jesus didn't choose a bride based on her beauty. He gave her beauty by choosing her.

Prayer

Jesus, thank You for loving me even when I felt unlovable. Thank You for washing me, clothing me, and calling me Yours. Help me reject the lies of shame and stand confidently in Your love—as a cherished part of Your radiant Bride.

Reflection Questions

1. Do you sometimes see yourself as unworthy of Christ's love? Why?

_____

_____

_____

_____

2. How does Ephesians 5:27 reshape the way you think about your identity as part of His Bride?

_____

_____

_____

_____

3. What would change if you believed Jesus actually delights in you?

_____

_____

_____

_____

_____

_____

_____

_____

_____

_____

_____

_____

_____

Day 19 – Is God Mad at Me Every Time I Sin?

Truth for Today: 1 Thessalonians 5:9

"For God did not appoint us to suffer wrath but to receive salvation through our Lord Jesus Christ."

It's a question many believers wrestle with: When I sin, is God mad at me? Disappointed? Ready to punish me?

We often imagine God as a moody Father—pleased when we're obedient, angry when we don't measure up. But that's not the gospel. That's religious fear. The truth is far more liberating.

The Bible says, "God did not appoint us to suffer wrath." Why? Because the full weight of God's wrath for your sin was poured out on Jesus. At the cross, Christ drank the entire cup of judgment—down to the last drop. There's no wrath left for you. None.

That means you'll never face a moment of divine anger or rejection. The wrath that once stood between you and God has been forever satisfied. When He looks at you, He doesn't see a sinner awaiting punishment but a son or daughter already embraced. The cross didn't just remove wrath—it secured your salvation through our Lord Jesus Christ.

Does that mean God ignores sin? No. Sin still grieves Him because He loves you. It distracts you from your true identity and purpose, wounds others, and pulls your attention away from the life Jesus bought for you. But God's response to your sin isn't anger—it's compassion, correction, and restoration. He doesn't punish His children—He disciplines them in love (Hebrews 12:6).

Imagine a parent whose child falls while learning to walk. The parent doesn't lash out—they rush in. That's God's passion toward you when you fall. His correction isn't rejection; it's proof of His love for you.

When you sin, the Holy Spirit doesn't condemn you—He reminds you of your true identity: you're in Christ, clothed in His righteousness, sealed by His Spirit, and forever His. You're not a slave trying to earn favor—you're a child already accepted.

Romans 5:1 says you have peace with God through Jesus. That peace doesn't dissolve when you fail. It's anchored in Christ's finished work, not your daily routine or performance.

So when you stumble, don't hide from God—run to Him. The cross already settled the matter of wrath. What remains now is help in your time of need, mercy in your time of misery, grace in your time of grief, and love in your time of loneliness.

Prayer

Father, thank You that I'm not under wrath but under grace. When I sin, remind me that Jesus took my judgment once for all. Help me trust in You, not try to run from You. Let me experience Your mercy in my weakness and rest in Your unchanging love.

Reflection Questions

1. Have you imagined God as angry or disappointed after you sin?

2. How does knowing Jesus already bore your judgment change your response to failure?

3. What does it look like to approach God with confidence rather than fear?

_____

_____

_____

_____

_____

_____

_____

_____

_____

_____

_____

_____

_____

Day 20 – Will God Tell Me, 'Depart from Me?'

Truth for Today: Matthew 7:23

"Then I will declare to them, 'I never knew you; depart from me, you workers of lawlessness.'"

---

ew verses stir more fear than this one: "Depart from Me." It's the nightmare scenario—standing before Jesus, only to be turned away. Many believers read Matthew 7:23 and wonder, Could this be me? What if I thought I was saved, but I wasn't?

Let's look at the context for clarity. Jesus is not speaking to those who trusted in Him. He's addressing people who trusted in their own religious works: "Did we not prophesy… cast out demons… do many mighty works in Your name?" Their confidence was in what they had done—not in who Jesus is or what He had done for them.

They used His name, but never knew Him. There was activity without relationship, work without wisdom. They were workers of lawlessness because they operated apart from the righteousness that only comes by faith.

Here's the key to the passage: If you are in Christ, this verse is not about you.

Jesus will never say, "Depart from Me," to someone He died to bring near. He doesn't reject those united to Him by faith. In fact, remember what Jesus said previously in John 10:28, "I give them eternal life, and they will never perish, and no one will snatch them out of my hand."

If you've trusted in Jesus—His death for your sin and His resurrection for your life—then you are known, and you belong to Him forever. He welcomed you the moment you believed, and He will never cast you out (John 6:37).

Satan wants you to live in fear of being disqualified. But the gospel brings assurance. You didn't earn your place in God's family by your works, so you can't lose it through weakness. Your salvation is anchored in Christ's finished work.

When you fail, when you doubt, when you feel like the worst Christian ever—God doesn't say, "Depart." He says, "Come." The cross removed every barrier. Your union with Christ is one spirit. You are kept, loved, and sealed forever.

Let Matthew 7:23 be a sober warning for the "self-righteous"—but not a source of fear for the loved and redeemed child of God.

Prayer

Jesus, thank You that I am known by You and secured by Your love. I don't trust in my works—I trust in Your grace and Your finished work. When fear creeps in, remind me that I am safe, secure, and that You never send away those who belong to You.

Reflection Questions

1. Have you ever feared being told, "Depart from Me"? What fueled that fear?

_____

_____

_____

_____

_____

2. What's the difference between knowing about Jesus and being known by Him?

_____

_____

_____

_____

_____

3. How does trusting in Jesus' work (instead of your own) give you assurance?

_____

_____

_____

_____

_____

_____

_____

_____

_____

_____

_____

_____

Day 21 – My Sins Run Too Deep and Wide

Truth for Today: Psalm 103:12

"As far as the east is from the west, so far has He removed our transgressions from us."

Some days, the weight of your past can feel crushing. You might think, If people knew the whole story… if God really saw it all, He couldn't possibly forgive me. Your sins feel too deep, too wide, too much to wash away.

But the gospel goes deeper than your worst day and wider than your biggest regret. It's greater than your failures and more faithful than your shame.

David—the man who wrote Psalm 103—knew what it meant to sin deeply. Adultery, deceit, and murder. And yet, he also came to know the mercy of God. He wrote that the Lord removes our transgressions "as far as the east is from the west"—an immeasurable, infinite distance.

That's not an exaggeration, it's simply the truth of the gospel. Why east and west? Because they never meet. When you travel north you will eventually be going south. But you can travel east forever and never go west! That's God's way of saying: Your sin is totally gone. Totally removed.

And that means God doesn't bring it back up. He doesn't replay the evidence or reopen the case. What's been removed has been forgotten in the depths of His mercy. You may still remember your sins, but God chooses not to. When He looks at you, He sees His righteous child. The blood of Jesus didn't just cover your past—it erased the record and declared you free forever.

When Jesus died, He didn't forgive some of your sins. He took all of them—past, present, and future—and nailed them to the cross. Your record is not on pause; it's wiped clean. Not because your sins weren't serious, but because His grace is greater than all of them.

Romans 5:20 says it like this: "Where sin increased, grace abounded all the more." The more sin, the more grace. Not to excuse it, but to assure the world: you are not beyond redemption no matter what you have done.

So if you're still haunted by what you've done, stop measuring your sin—and start meditating on your Savior. Snap that measuring stick over your knee! Your forgiveness isn't based on the size of your mess, but on the size of your Savior and the power of His blood.

And His blood has spoken: "Paid in full."

Prayer

Father, thank You that no sin is too deep and no past too wide for Your mercy. Thank You for removing my transgressions completely. Help me live from this truth—free from shame, and full of gratitude for Your amazing grace.

Reflection Questions

1. Do you sometimes believe your sins are "too much" for God to forgive? Why?

_____

_____

_____

_____

_____

_____

2. How does Psalm 103:12 reshape your view of God's mercy?

_____

_____

_____

_____

_____

3. What would it look like to live as someone whose sin has been truly removed?

_____

_____

_____

_____

_____

_____

_____

_____

_____

_____

_____

_____

_____

_____

Day 22 – Am I a Hypocrite?

Truth for Today: Hebrews 12:4

"In your struggle against sin you have not yet resisted to the point of shedding your blood."

---

*H*ave you ever felt like a fraud in your faith? Like you're saying one thing but doing another—worshiping on Sunday but stumbling by Monday? That quiet voice creeps in: Am I a hypocrite?

But there's a difference between hypocrisy and struggle.

A hypocrite pretends to be a "good person" while living a sinful lifestyle. A believer mourns his struggle with sin and longs to walk free from it—even while wrestling with temptation. If you hate sin and are walking with Jesus, you're not a hypocrite, you're a new creation learning to walk and grow in His grace.

Is an infant born with the ability to walk? Of course not. So give yourself some room to grow, learn to crawl, learn to walk, learn to run. Not as an excuse for sin, but as an invitation to stop condemning yourself. You're learning. You're growing. And God's grace makes room for both.

Hebrews says,

> *"In your struggle against sin, you have not yet*
> *resisted to the point of shedding your blood."*

That's not condemning—it's a reminder. Your struggle isn't hypocrisy—it's evidence of the battle. Jesus resisted sin to death for you and in your place on the cross. He went all the way—shedding His blood to set you free!

We all struggle, but the moment you trusted Christ, you were made righteous. Your transformation is still unfolding. Old desires don't disappear overnight, transformation happens over time. New desires may feel weak or slow to develop. But that's learning and growing. That doesn't mean your faith is fake. It means you're still dependent on God's grace.

The enemy whispers, "You're a fraud." But God says, "You're mine. I began this good work, and I will finish it." (Philippians 1:6)

So you don't have to live in seclusion. Faith weakens in secrecy, but maturity grows in transparency. Admitting your weakness is not spiritual failure—it's a sign that the Spirit is at work in you.

Jesus didn't come for the polished and perfect. He came for the broken, the weak, and the weary—the ones who know they need Him. If you're struggling—but looking to Jesus—then you're not a hypocrite. You're being molded into a masterpiece!

Prayer

Father, thank You for Your grace in my weakness. Thank You that my struggles don't disqualify me—they remind me of Jesus' shed blood that drew me close when I was far off. Teach me to walk with thanksgiving, resting in Your love and not my performance.

Reflection Questions

1. Have you ever confused spiritual struggle with hypocrisy?

_____

_____

_____

_____

2. How does Hebrews 12:4 challenge or encourage your view of struggling with sin?

_____

_____

_____

_____

3. What would it look like to walk in the light without fear or pretense?

_____

_____

_____

_____

_____

_____

_____

_____

_____

_____

_____

_____

_____

Day 23

Day 23 – But I'm Not a "Prayer Warrior"

Truth for Today: Luke 18:1

"Then Jesus told his disciples a parable to show them that they should always pray and not give up."

Many believers admire those who seem to pray with passion and consistency—often called "prayer warriors." You might look at them and think, I'm just not wired that way. I don't pray like that. And maybe I'm not a strong Christian because of it.

But here's the good news: You don't need to be a "prayer warrior" to be heard by God because prayer isn't your life; Christ is your life! Your confidence doesn't come from how you pray, but from who you belong to.

You're not heard because you pray perfectly—you're heard because Jesus perfectly obeyed. The One who taught you to pray also opened the way for you to be heard. His righteousness gives you full access to the Father.

In Luke 18, Jesus tells a parable about a persistent widow who keeps returning to an unjust judge until he finally gives her justice. Jesus wasn't highlighting her skill or eloquence—He was showing the power of persistence, to "always pray and never give up."

89   Rooted in Christ

Jesus wasn't pointing to human strength but to divine grace. He knew we'd grow weary, distracted, and discouraged, yet He gave us this story so we'd remember—God is not an unjust judge, but a loving Father who listens to His children.

Prayer isn't a performance; it's a relationship. It's less about your ability and more about your connection with the Father, Son, and Holy Spirit. God isn't moved by fancy words or impressive speeches. He delights when you simply come to Him—honestly, dependently, and even imperfectly.

Some days, prayer may feel dry or difficult. Other days, it might flow with gratitude and joy. That's okay. What matters most is that you come—as you are. No pressure. Not perfect. Just present.

You don't have to compare yourself to others. Your prayers matter because you are God's child. And when you don't know what to say, the Spirit Himself intercedes for you with groanings too deep for words (Romans 8:26).

So keep communicating. Keep praying. And remember that "Prayer Warrior" is never mentioned in the Bible anyway. Even when you can't find the words, Jesus is interceding for you (Hebrews 7:25). The Spirit Himself prays on your behalf (Romans 8:26).

Prayer

Father, thank You that You hear me even when my prayers feel distant or few. Help me to come to You with confidence, knowing that You care more about my heart than my words. Help me to pray without pressure by simply coming into Your presence and sharing my heart.

Reflection Questions

1. Have you felt discouraged about your "prayer life" when comparing yourself to others?

_____

_____

_____

_____

_____

2. What does Luke 18:1 teach you about God's desire for ongoing prayer?

_____

_____

_____

_____

_____

3. How can you pray in a way that's real, rather than perfect?

_____

_____

_____

_____

_____

_____

_____

_____

_____

_____

_____

_____

Day 24 – Do I Spend Enough Time with God?

Truth for Today: Psalm 61:3

"O God, you are my God; earnestly I seek you; my soul thirsts for you; my flesh faints for you, as in a dry and weary land where there is no water."

$\mathcal{I}$t's a common question among believers: Am I spending enough time with God? You may measure time by minutes or hours, wondering if your quiet moments, prayers, or Bible reading add up. Maybe you feel guilty when life gets busy and your "devotional time" shrinks.

But the heart behind the question matters more than the clock.

David's prayer in Psalm 63 reveals a deep hunger and thirst for God—not a checklist of religious duty. He earnestly seeks the Lord because his soul is parched without Him. It's not about meeting a daily quota, but about a genuine longing to know and enjoy the Lord.

Time with God isn't about perfection or quantity—it's about connection. And here's the truth: you're always spending time with God, because He lives in you and you in Him. Because of Christ's finished work, God doesn't just meet you in quiet moments—He lives in you 24/7/365.

That constant presence isn't something you earn—it's something Jesus secured. When He cried out, "It is finished," the veil in the temple tore from top to bottom (Matthew 27:51), symbolizing that the barrier between God and man was gone forever. Through His blood, you've been brought near, adopted, and made a dwelling place for His Spirit.

Sometimes the busyness of life makes it feel impossible to slow down. Yet God meets you where you are—in that still small voice, a whispered prayer, a Bible passage that comes to mind, or just with the peace of knowing He's walking with you. You don't need a formal "quiet time" to be in His presence. He's already present with you.

Jesus said in John 15:4, "Abide in me, and I in you." Abiding is more than scheduled minutes. It's Him living in you, a continual dependence, a loving relationship where you remain connected to the One who gave you His life.

So don't measure your faith with a clock—or with a ruler. And if you are, go ahead and snap that ruler in half. God isn't measuring you that way. He delights in you because of Christ, not because of your measuring stick or performance.

The gospel isn't about how much time you spend pursuing God—it's about how relentlessly He pursued you. Jesus didn't wait for you to draw near; He stepped into your weary world, bore your sin, and rose again so that intimacy with God would never depend on your effort again. He invited you into a relationship, not into a ritual.

Prayer

Father, thank You that You are always with me. Help me not to focus on the minutes I log, but on the nearness of Your presence. Teach me to walk with You, rest in You, and enjoy You—throughout every moment of my day.

Reflection Questions

1. How do you usually measure your "time with God"?

_____

_____

_____

_____

_____

2. What would it look like to walk with God instead of counting the hours?

_____

_____

_____

_____

_____

3. How can you stay in communion with Him throughout your day?

_____

_____

_____

_____

_____

_____

_____

_____

_____

_____

_____

_____

_____

Day 25

Day 25 – The Wages of Sin vs. The Gift of God

Truth for Today: Romans 6:23

"For the wages of sin is death, but the free gift of God is eternal life in Christ Jesus our Lord."

The message of the Bible is clear: sin earns the rightful wages of death. This is not just physical death, but spiritual separation from God—the ultimate consequence of unbelief in Him.

However, grace is the unearned, undeserved favor of God. Grace is God stepping in where law fails, offering life instead of death. Romans 6:23 contrasts the wages we earn, with the gift God freely gives: eternal life through Jesus Christ.

Every sin carries a cost, and justice demands it be paid in full. But God, rich in mercy, stepped into our courtroom, and instead of handing down the sentence we earned, He nailed the hands of His Son to a cross. Jesus didn't negotiate a lesser punishment—He took the full penalty of sin so that grace could be truly free for us.

Grace means that even though you've broken the law and earned the wages of death, God offers you a full pardon, a new life, and the Spirit who will guide you into all truth. (John 16:13).

All because of what Jesus did on the cross. He took your death sentence upon Himself so you could receive His life. This gift is not something you earn by following rules or trying harder. It's received by faith. It frees you from the burden of legalism and a fear of punishment.

The wages of sin being death shows God's seriousness against sin, and the grace of God that meets our needs perfectly. It changes your standing before God from condemned to justified, from lost to found.

Living under grace doesn't mean ignoring the wages of sin. It means looking at the One who paid for them with His blood. Jesus didn't just cover a debt like some bill collector—He paid with His life, taking the lashes to His back, the nails to His hands, and the piercing of His feet.

And you? You walked away free, forgiven—and without a scratch. That's the scandal and beauty of grace—it cost Jesus everything and you nothing. He took your wages so you could receive His wealth. The gospel isn't a transaction; it was a transfer. His death became your life, His punishment became your pardon, and His resurrection began your transformation.

Prayer

Father, thank You that Your grace is greater than the law of death. Help me live in the freedom and joy of Your gift, not in the fear of punishment. Help me to walk in Your love, full of Your grace, and empowered by Your Spirit.

Reflection Questions

1. How does this free gift inspire you today?

_____

_____

_____

_____

_____

2. What difference does it make to know eternal life is a gift, not a wage?

_____

_____

_____

_____

_____

3. How can grace shape your daily life differently than fear or duty?

_____

_____

_____

_____

_____

_____

_____

_____

_____

_____

_____

_____

_____

Day 26 – I Feel Unaccepted in God's Sight

Truth for Today: Romans 15:7

"Therefore welcome one another as Christ has welcomed you, for the glory of God."

$\mathcal{I}$t's a painful and lonely feeling—believing that God doesn't fully accept you. Maybe you've felt distant, rejected, or unworthy to approach Him. The thought creeps in: If He really knew me—all of me—He wouldn't love me or want me near. But the truth is, He already knows you—and still welcomes you.

Romans 15:7 calls us to welcome one another just as Christ has welcomed us. It's not partial or polite. It's personal, wholehearted, and permanent welcome. Jesus doesn't wait until you're cleaned up or fixed—He welcomes you just as you are.

And when He welcomes you, He also restores your sense of belonging. You're not a guest who might overstay their welcome—you're a child who belongs in the Father's house. His arms remain open, His table always set, and His presence always available.

Your acceptance by God isn't based on your performance or how well you follow *the rules*. It's based solely on

Christ's finished work. He embraced you the moment you put your faith in Him. You are welcomed, adopted, and loved—not just barely tolerated.

Feelings of rejection often stem from shame, past failures, or a distorted view of God. But the gospel is so much better. God does not reject sinners who come to Him in faith—He welcomes them. Jesus dined with tax collectors, forgave adulterers, and touched lepers. He pursued the outcasts, not because they were worthy, but because He came to seek and save the lost.

When you feel unaccepted, don't look to your own understanding. Look to Christ. He says, "Come to me, all who are weary and burdened, and I will give you rest." That invitation is still open. Your flaws and failures don't disqualify you—they become the very place where grace meets you.

Even when your emotions scream rejection, let your heart be anchored in truth. The cross is God's final word about your acceptance—written not in ink, but in blood. You're not striving for approval; you're standing in it.

Your acceptance isn't based on your faithfulness, but on His. The gospel assures you that you are welcomed into God's presence—and seated at His right hand, not as a servant or stranger, but as His beloved child. Even when your feelings waver, God's truth stands. He doesn't just accept you—He delights in you because you belong to Jesus.

Prayer

Father, thank You that You welcome me fully through Jesus. When I feel ashamed or unworthy, help me reject the lies and stand in the truth of Your grace. Teach me to live in the joy of being Your accepted, beloved child—not by my merit, but by Christ's finished work.

Reflection Questions

1. When have you felt unaccepted by God?

_____

_____

_____

_____

_____

_____

2. What thoughts or lies fueled that feeling? How does Romans 15:7 reshape your view of God's welcome?

_____

_____

_____

_____

_____

3. What would change if you truly believed God
    delights in welcoming you every day?

_____

_____

_____

_____

_____

_____

_____

_____

_____

_____

_____

Day 27 – Should I Be Afraid of Hell?

Truth for Today: John 5:24

"Truly, truly, I say to you, whoever hears my word and believes Him who sent me has eternal life. He does not come into judgment but has passed from death to life."

The fear of hell can be paralyzing. It creeps in during unexpected moments or after falling—whispering doubts about your salvation and suggesting that maybe, just maybe, you're not safe after all.

But Jesus offers clarity, not confusion. In John 5:24, He gives a stunning promise: "Whoever hears my word and believes… has eternal life. He does not come into judgment but has passed from death to life." That's not just a possibility—it's a present, permanent reality.

If you've believed in Christ, you're not waiting for eternal life to begin someday. You have it now. You've already crossed over from death to life. You don't need to wonder if you'll end up condemned—you've already been redeemed.

Jesus didn't die so His followers would live in fear of hell. He died to set us free from guilt and the curse of sin. The judgment you deserved has already fallen—on Him. The wrath of God was fully satisfied at the cross.

When Jesus cried out, "It is finished," He was declaring your debt canceled, your record wiped out, and your life changed. The grave couldn't hold Him, and because you are in Him, it can't hold you. His resurrection is your proof that death has been defeated and hell has lost its claim on you.

So what remains for the believer? Not punishment, but peace. Not dread, but delight in God. The Holy Spirit doesn't lead you by fear of hell; He assures you of your adoption. He reminds you that you belong, that you're sealed, and that nothing can separate you from God's love.

Yes, hell is real. But if you are in Christ, it's no longer your destination. You are not on trial. The verdict has already been declared: righteous, forgiven, and alive forever in Him. So don't live in the fear of judgment. Live in the warmth of His love, grace, mercy, and life.

Prayer

Father, thank You for the clear promise of eternal life in Jesus. Help me believe that I've already passed from death to life. When fear rises, remind me of Your Word and of the cross. Let my heart rest in the truth that I am safe in You forever.

Reflection Questions

1. Have you struggled with a lingering fear of hell, even after trusting in Christ?

_____

_____

_____

_____

_____

_____

2. How does John 5:24 change the way you understand your eternal security?

_____

_____

_____

_____

_____

_____

3. What would it look like to live with joyful confidence instead of fear?

_____

_____

_____

_____

_____

_____

_____

_____

_____

_____

_____

_____

_____

Day 28 – Holy and Blameless

Truth for Today: Ephesians 1:4

"For he chose us in him before the creation of the world to be holy and blameless in his sight."

$\mathcal{S}$ometimes it feels impossible to believe that God sees you as holy and blameless. Your mistakes, regrets, and failures crowd your mind. You might wonder, How can I be holy when I still struggle? How can I be blameless when I fall short so often?

Before God created the world, He chose you in Christ to be holy and blameless. That means your identity in God's eyes was established long before your life began. This isn't about what you've done—it's about what Christ has done for you and in you.

At the cross, your old life was crucified with Him, and through His resurrection, a new life began. Holiness isn't something you're trying to achieve—it's about Christ who now lives in you.

Jesus lived a perfect, holy, blameless life that you couldn't. He took all your blame and wore your shame, naked, exposed, and humiliated. He bore your guilt and punishment. And in exchange, He gave you His righteousness. This is the great gospel exchange—your sin for His purification.

Now, when God looks at you, He sees you in Christ. Not stained by your past, but clothed in His righteousness. That's what it means to be "holy and blameless in His sight."

This isn't a temporary label that depends on how well you behave. It's permanent, sealed by Christ's blood, and guaranteed by His resurrection. Even when your daily walk feels exhausting or messy, your position in Him remains holy and blameless.

"Holy" means you are set apart—not because you're sinless, but because He has made you His. "Blameless" means you are without accusation—not because you never fail, but because Jesus took the blame for you.

So when guilt whispers, when shame returns, when the enemy accuses, remember, God sees you in Christ.

You didn't earn this identity, and you can't lose it. It was God's gift, Christ's work, and your inheritance. Let that truth reshape how you face your struggles, respond to failure, and walk forward in faith.

Prayer

Father, thank You that You chose me before the foundation of the world. Thank You that through Jesus, I am holy and blameless in Your sight. Help me live in this truth—not striving to earn Your love, but walking in the freedom of Your grace. Teach me to see myself as You do—redeemed, cleansed, and set apart in Christ.

Reflection Questions

1. How do you usually view yourself before God—through your mistakes or His grace?

_____

_____

_____

_____

_____

2. What does it mean to you that God chose you to be holy and blameless before the world was made?

_____

_____

_____

_____

_____

3. How can this truth reshape your thinking in moments of guilt or defeat?

Day 29 – Adopted and Loved

Truth for Today: Ephesians 1:5

"In love He predestined us for adoption to sonship through Jesus Christ, in accordance with His pleasure and will."

---

ew truths are more tender—or more transforming—than this: God didn't just forgive you; He adopted you. You were not only rescued from sin's penalty—you were welcomed into a family. The gospel is not merely a courtroom verdict of "Not guilty," but a homecoming invitation that says, "You belong to Me."

Before you took your first breath, before the world began, God's plan was already in motion: to make you His child through Jesus Christ. Adoption wasn't His backup plan—it was His pleasure and will. He wanted you.

In the ancient world, adoption carried great honor. An adopted child received full legal standing, inheritance, and identity in the family. Nothing could undo it. Ephesians uses that image to help us grasp what God has done through Christ. You have been given the rights, privileges, and name of a true son or daughter of the King.

On the cross, Jesus took the judgment you deserved so that you could receive the relationship He deserved. He was forsaken for a moment so you could be embraced forever. He wore a crown of thorns so you could wear a crown of sonship. The Father's plan of adoption was signed in the blood of His Son.

Now, the Holy Spirit lives within you as the Spirit of adoption, crying out "Abba, Father!" (Romans 8:15). It's the Spirit reminding you that you are loved and wanted. You no longer have to approach God as a distant judge, but as a devoted Father.

When shame whispers that you're unworthy, when guilt says you don't belong, remember whose family name you carry. Your place is not earned by performance but sealed by grace. You've been given a seat at the table, an inheritance in heaven, and a Father who delights in you.

Adoption means you are never alone, never orphaned, and never forgotten. The same Father who chose you will never let you go. His love began before time and will outlast eternity.

Prayer

Father, thank You that You didn't just save me from sin—you adopted me into Your family. Thank You for calling me Your child, giving me Your name, and delighting in me through Jesus. When I doubt my worth or drift into fear, remind me that I am fully accepted, loved, and secure as Your child.

Reflection Questions

1. What does spiritual adoption reveal about God's heart toward you?

_____

_____

_____

_____

_____

2. How does knowing you're a beloved son or daughter affect the way you pray and live?

_____

_____

_____

_____

_____

3. When feelings of unworthiness arise, what truths
    remind you that you belong?

_____

_____

_____

_____

_____

_____

_____

_____

_____

_____

_____

_____

_____

_____

Day 30 – Nothing Can Separate Us

Truth for Today: Romans 8:38–39

"For I am convinced that neither death nor life, neither angels nor demons, neither the present nor the future, nor any powers... will be able to separate us from the love of God that is in Christ Jesus our Lord."

---

*Y*ou are not who you used to be. You are no longer a slave to sin, under the law, or condemned. Because of Jesus' finished work on the cross—and His victorious resurrection—you are forgiven, made new, raised, and seated with Him. You are eternally secure in the love of God.

Romans 8 closes with one of the most triumphant declarations in all of Scripture: *"Nothing can separate us from the love of God in Christ Jesus."* Not your past, not your present, not even your failures or fears. This is the final word on your identity: you belong to Christ—forever.

This entire journey—from sin to salvation, from striving to resting, from guilt to grace—finds its completion in this truth: you are in Christ, and that means you are secure, free, and deeply loved. Jesus didn't give you temporary life; He gave you His life—eternal and unbreakable. The same Spirit who raised Him from the dead now lives in you, empowering you daily. Every day becomes a testimony of resurrection power. Even when you stumble, His life in you never fades, and His love for you never fails. Your failures can't undo His forgiveness, and your weakness can't reverse His work. You are kept, carried, and made complete in the love of Christ.

God didn't just save you *from* something—He saved you *for* something. You've been bought with a price, rescued from death, and redeemed for life so you can walk in freedom and share the hope of Christ with others. The gospel begins with forgiveness but doesn't end there—it launches you into a lifetime of love, joy, and peace.

So don't hold back. You don't need to fear judgment or strive for approval. You don't have to prove yourself. Walk in the confidence of one who cannot be separated from His love, and live as one changed by grace. Let your life become a living picture of the gospel—offering the same mercy you've received. The new life God began in you is only the beginning of eternity's story. Grace brought you home, and love will keep you there.

And never forget: nothing—absolutely nothing—can separate you from the love of God in Christ Jesus.

Prayer

Father, thank You for Your unconditional love through Christ, and that nothing can separate me from Him. Help me walk in the freedom You've given me, and boldly share the good news of Your grace with the world.

Reflection Questions

1. What truth from this devotional series has impacted you most deeply?

_____

_____

_____

_____

_____

2. How does Romans 8:38–39 speak to your fears, doubts, or struggles?

_____

_____

_____

_____

_____

3. What does it mean for you to live free, forgiven, and truly loved?

_____

_____

_____

_____

_____

_____

_____

_____

_____

_____

_____

_____

_____

_____

Afterword – Rooted Forever in Christ

This 30-day journey was never about self-improvement—it's about gospel transformation. Every truth you've read points to one reality: you are in Christ, and Christ is in you. You are loved, chosen, forgiven, raised, seated, and therefore Rooted in Christ. The same grace that saved you will sustain you until the day you see Him face to face.

Stay rooted and grounded. Keep watering your soul in His Word and resting in His love. When storms come, remember—you are planted in unshakable soil. You don't grow by trying harder; you grow by learning who Christ is and who you are in Him. Let the roots of His truth hold you fast, and let the fruit of His Spirit show His love to the world through your life.

May you walk forward confidently in this unchanging truth: nothing can separate you from the love of God that is in Christ Jesus our Lord.

Other Books by Erick Hurt

Coming Soon

- **Faith Under Fire:** A 30-Day Devotional for First Responders

- **This is Real Love:** A 30-Day Devotional on True Love

- **Is This the End?:** A 30-Day Devotional for Those who have Lost Loved Ones

- **Be Sober Minded:** A 30-Day Devotional on Transforming Your Mind

For more updates, visit ErickHurt.com.

Invitation

If this devotional has encouraged you, I'd love to hear from you. How is God working in your life? How has this devotional blessed you? How can I pray for you or serve you?

Your story matters. Your testimony of God's grace could be the encouragement someone else needs to keep going. Feel free to share your thoughts, prayer requests, or what God is doing in your life—I'd be honored to listen, pray, and celebrate with you.

Group Leader's Guide: Rooted In Christ

Purpose of the Group

To anchor believers in the truth of the gospel, renew their identity in Christ, and help them walk in daily gospel freedom—together.

How to Use This Devotional in a Group

1. Weekly Gatherings (Recommended)
- Meet once a week to discuss the 7 devotionals from that week.

- Choose a quiet space where everyone can share comfortably.

2. Everyone Reads Daily
- Group members read one devotional each day (30 days total).

- Encourage members to write in their books—prayers, notes, and reflections.

3. Focus on Jesus
- Each session is centered on the finished work of Christ.

- Help participants see how every lesson points to Him—His death, resurrection, and their new life in Him.

Suggested Weekly Group Format (60–75 minutes)

1. Welcome & Prayer (5 minutes)

Begin with a warm welcome and a short prayer. Ask God to guide your time together.

2. Check-In (10–15 minutes)

Ask each person to share briefly how the week went and how the devotionals impacted them.
Example question: "What truth encouraged or challenged you this week?"

3. Scripture Focus (10 minutes)

Choose one or two key Scriptures from the past week's devotionals. Read them aloud together and ask what stood out or how they point to Christ.

4. Group Discussion (25–30 minutes)

Use the core discussion questions below to guide conversation. Encourage honesty, listening, and gospel-centered sharing.

5. Application & Prayer (15 minutes)

Close by asking: "How can we pray for you?" Spend time praying for one another, focusing on gospel hope, freedom, and transformation.

Core Discussion Questions (repeat weekly)

1. What truth stood out most to you this week?

2. Where did you feel challenged, or encouraged?

3. How did the gospel become more real to you?

4. What is God inviting you to give up or believe?

5. How can we pray for you this week?

Leader Encouragement

You and I are not the experts—Jesus is. Be a good listener, quick to listen and slow to speak. Try not to be a fixer. Stay focused on the gospel, not behavior change. The goal is heart transformation through the finished work of Christ.